BEYOND THE
KITCHEN

ISBN: 9781073755141

Published by Movement Publishing
Printed in the United States of America.

BEYOND THE
KITCHEN

HOW TO COOK UP SUCCESS WITH LIFE'S MISTAKES

Nigel Mushambi

Shane Mushambi

Mistakes aren't failures, they are growth plates for learning.

2 BROTHERS IN THE KITCHEN

DEDICATION

We dedicate this book to our Mom, for always having our backs and teaching us how to run a business; you are amazing, "THANK YOU." To our Dad, for all the late night runs to get ingredients; we are forever grateful. To Aunt Tina, for being our biggest cheerleader; you are spectacular. To Grandma Carrie, for inspiring us to start baking; all we can say is "THANK YOU." And finally to our Extended Sienna Family for supporting our baking dreams, Thank you. You guys are AWESOME.

TABLE OF CONTENTS

INTRODUCTION

Shane and Nigel Mushambi own a successful baking business called 2 Brothers in the Kitchen (2BrosITK). They boast a corporate client list that includes universities, medical establishments, and financial institutions. They are endorsed by many professional groups, including Vision Investing Partners, LLC, an investment club, and McHughson, LLC, a computer software development and applications business.

Their desserts are in high demand. They offer cupcakes in several flavors, cake jars, cakesicles, custom designed cakes for a variety of events, ranging from weddings to birthdays, and many other sweet treats.

Despite their many successes, which not only include economic achievements and philanthropic support of organizations in the United States and Zimbabwe, they have made their fair share of critical mistakes. They know firsthand the agony of failure, the frustration of trying to reach perfection but missing the mark by a sliver, and the disappointment of defeat.

At times, they wanted to quit. During frustrating moments when their cakes cracked or failed, and they had to keep baking, sometimes until two o'clock in the morning, the pressure became almost too much to bear. But somehow, they kept going.

These young icons found a way to turn their mistakes into valuable lessons for others. Join Shane and Nigel as they journey through their last couple of years of ups and downs. Learn from them and be inspired.

CHAPTER 1

THE PUNISHMENT

Friday afternoon around 1:00

Shane and Nigel's mom stood in the middle of the kitchen and surveyed the growing pile of dishes in the sink. She also noticed that the trash was so high, it had begun to spill over onto the floor.

What's going on? She thought to herself. *I told Shane to wash the dishes. Nigel hasn't emptied the trash in two days. I can't even do the laundry because the boys' socks and T-shirts are still in the washing machine. Where are they anyway? Why aren't they cleaning the kitchen as I told them to do?*

She heard the familiar sounds of "clickity clack" coming from the game room upstairs. Her sons were playing those darn video games again.

The game room door suddenly flew open. Stunned, Shane and Nigel dropped their controllers and turned to see their mom glaring at them. They exchanged nervous glances. They both knew they were in BIG trouble.

"Uh oh," Nigel whispered.

"Hey, Mom. We were just about to…" Shane began.

"You weren't *just about* to do anything," their mom interrupted. "You two have been in this game room all day long." She scanned the room and noticed that, just like in the kitchen, the trash can was overflowing with what looked like a mixture of empty soda cans, chip bags, crumpled notebook paper, and pencil shavings. She reached in the trash can and retrieved one of the balls of paper. She unraveled it and held it up for Nigel to see. "Are you done with your science report?" she asked.

"Not yet, but it's not due until next week."

"I asked you to finish your rough draft tonight. I didn't ask when it was due." She let out a deep sigh and then continued. "I have had it with you dragging your feet until the last minute. And look around this game room; And the kitchen! This is way beyond ludicrous. Turn that game off right now and head to the kitchen. There are piles of dishes in the sink and, Nigel, you still haven't folded your laundry from two days ago."

"Mom," Shane pleaded, "Just three more minutes and we'll turn it off. We promise. Please, Mom. We're in the middle of a game, and if we shut down, we will lose everything."

"Shane Mushambi, I won't ask again. Matter of fact, disconnect everything right now. This is ridiculous! I'm fed up with you two constantly playing video games and not focusing on things that really matter. I want it all, the games, the Xbox, the controllers and none of it will be returned until you two show some sense of responsibility around here."

"But Mom…" Nigel protested.

"Since you are obviously having trouble understanding me, give me your phones too."

Shane and Nigel froze and stared at their mom in disbelief. They were both afraid to speak.

"Hand them over, now!" she scolded.

They knew they would not be able to come to an amicable agreement with their mom, so both boys handed over their phones.

"Thank you," she said. "Now, to make sure I get my point across, no electronics this entire weekend. You will spend the weekend catching up on your chores. Based on the looks of this room, you will be in here for a while." She turned her attention to Nigel. "And you, you will finish working on your science paper."

"What are we going to do after we finish our chores?" Nigel implored.

"You figure it out. But no electronics this weekend. That means, no TV, no phones, no Xbox, and no computer unless you're researching your science paper and Shane, your history paper on the Middle Ages."

"Yes, ma'am," they both mumbled in unison.

As their mom turned to walk out of the room, she saw her husband standing in the doorway.

"Everything okay?" He asked.

"Not at all," she responded. "Your sons seem to think playing video games is more important than getting their schoolwork, chores, and everything else that matters, done. I'm tired of being nice. I've been more than fair. I realize they have a lot on their plates with baking and processing orders, but with success comes responsibility. If they're going to maintain their business, they have to do better. I mean, look at this place." She pointed to an overflowing trash can in the corner of the room. "They haven't done their laundry, cleaned the kitchen, or emptied a single trash can in the whole house. More importantly, they have school assignments that are due soon, and they should not be procrastinating."

Shane and Nigel's dad threw his hands up in surrender to his wife's disappointment. She made good sense. He turned to his sons and said, "I am as well disappointed in both of you guys. Shut it down now." He turned and left his sons to contend with their mother's wrath.

She stood in the doorway as the boys unplugged their Xbox and wrapped the cords around their controllers. "Awe, man!" Nigel said as he pounded his fist on his desk.

Shane whispered to Nigel, "How much do you want to bet, there're only like two dishes in the sink?"

"Twenty bucks!" Nigel said with confidence.

"Bet," Shane answered with a half-smile.

They spent the rest of their Friday afternoon scrubbing and cleaning. Angrily, they worked in silence. Just in case their mom added to their to-do lists, they avoided making eye contact with her. Both boys walked away in a somber mood and began catching up on a week's worth of chores.

When Shane and Nigel were done, they went back to Nigel's room.

"What do you want to do now?" Shane asked Nigel.

"What can we do?" Nigel shot back. "Mom took everything away." He turned on his laptop. "I might as well start working on my science paper."

"Okay. I'm going to my room to draw," Shane replied. However, his feet didn't move. "Nigel, do you remember when I was making that cake, and the flour flew all over the kitchen counter and floor?"

Nigel laughed so hard tears began to stream down his face. "Yes, I remember," he said as he struggled to catch his breath in between laughs. "It's funny now, but it wasn't so funny then. It took us over thirty minutes to clean up that flour-bomb. Do you remember when …?"

CHAPTER 2

INTEGRITY

*"Remember when we had to bake that German Chocolate cake **three** times..."*

"What in the world is going on with this cake?" Clearly, Shane was annoyed with the appearance of their cake as he removed it from the oven.

"What? What's wrong with it?" Nigel stuttered as he stretched his neck to get a better look from across the room. "Looks okay to me."

"Yeah, right. You can't even see the cake from over there. This cake looks like it scraped its knee. Dude, you *always* say our cakes look okay."

Nigel chuckled at his brother's comment and walked across the room to catch a glimpse of the cake. "Oh...You're right. Hmm... I don't know why it looks so *flaky*. I followed the recipe."

"Did you remember the butter?" Shane asked.

"Uh-huh," Nigel said.

"Did you melt the chocolate blocks before adding it to the batter?" Shane interrogated Nigel with a condescending tone.

Irritated with his brother's line of questioning, Nigel scrunched his lips together and gave Shane a 'side-eye.' "Yes, I followed the recipe," he responded sharply.

"Well, we have to trash it."

"Yeah, I guess you're right," Nigel uttered as he picked up the cake and chucked it in the trash. Afterward, he added, "I'll get the ingredients ready, and you start prepping the pans."

An hour later, Shane took the second cake out of the oven. "What is going on?" he yelled. "This is crazy. It's still too flaky!"

"I don't know why," Nigel said with a defeated tone in his voice. "Any way we can fix it? Can we just put a chocolate glaze over the cake? If we have to bake this cake a third time, we won't make any profit. We will actually lose money. We've used this German Chocolate recipe over ten times before and we have NEVER had any trouble with it."

"Humph! I know, but we don't have a choice," Shane said solemnly. "We just can't cover up the cake. How would you feel if someone gave you a flaky disaster? We have to get it right the next time. The client will be here in three hours, which isn't a lot of time considering, all we have to do. We have to prep the pans, bake the cake, and the cake has to cool down before we icing it."

"*And* we have to clean the kitchen," Nigel added as he looked around at the flour on the floor and sugar scattered all over the kitchen island. *Okay, Nigel, think!* He closed his eyes and devised a plan in his mind. "I'll get all the wet ingredients out, and you get the dry ones. Let's put everything on this side of the counter. I will start cleaning while you get the cake in the oven," Nigel instructed.

"Okay," Shane replied as he walked over to where they kept the flour and sugar canisters. He noticed an open bag of flour sitting right next to the canisters. "Nigel! Is this the flour you've been using?" he said with a puzzled look.

"Yeah," Nigel replied as he placed the eggs in a bowl of warm water to get them up to room temperature.

"This has got to be it!" Shane responded excitedly. "This is what's been making our cakes come out crazy looking. We have never used this type of flour before. Not only that...."

"I hope you're right," Nigel replied, interrupting Shane's long and drawn out explanation of why the flour had to be the culprit of the last two cake fails.

"Nigel, Nigel, NIGEL!" Shane voiced to get his brother's full attention. "Start whipping those eggs so we can get this cake in the oven."

Nigel ignored his brother's pestering.

The boys finished making the cake without saying a word. The only sounds that could be heard coming from the kitchen where an occasional "Plip. Plop," of water dripping from the faucet onto the pans in the sink and a whirring sound coming from the mixer.

Shane put the cake in the oven and started to wipe down the kitchen counters.

"We should be through with cleaning by the time the cake is done," Nigel said, breaking the silence.

Definition: Integrity is being truthful and holding yourself accountable when no one's watching. *Shane and I could have simply covered the German Chocolate cake with glaze, but that would have been dishonest on our part.*

Edible Thought: Lying, even by omission, is like chopping off the head of a hydra, a three-headed dragon. Every time you cut off its head, it grows three more. Thus, you may solve one problem by lying, but you will create additional problems.

CHAPTER 3

BE READY!

"Remember when we went to an event and we didn't have a credit card swiper..."

Nigel stared into the bathroom mirror and examined his outfit. *Hmm,* he thought to himself as he straightened his basketball print bowtie, *looking good. Perfect for a red-carpet event.*

"I'm excited," Shane said as he combed and patted down his hot-pink flat top. "Our first vending event: A private gala with over a hundred guests. It's a huge night for us. Are you nervous?" Shane reached for a hand mirror and checked the back of his hair.

"Not really," Nigel answered as he continued checking himself out.

"Okay, you two debonaire gents. It's time to rock and roll," their mom called out. "Let's go!"

***

They anticipated a magical night filled with glitz and glamour under the glistening lights that sparkled from the glass chandeliers. Shane and Nigel gleamed with excitement as they studied the ballroom. They listened to the various sounds of buzzing as the technical crew conducted their final sound check, and busy staff carefully placed fine china and silver eating utensils at each setting. They spotted award-winning food and lifestyle blogger, Cynthia Smoot, talking with Alanna Sarabia from *Good Morning Texas*. All of a sudden, Shane and Nigel began to feel a little nervous.

A hostess led them to where they would be setting up their dessert table. They raised their *2BrosITK* step and repeat banner, and positioned it in front of a wall.

"Shane, you start putting the cake jars on that three-tier stand," their mom instructed.

"Ok," Shane responded. "Nigel, can you help me?"

"Sure," Nigel answered as he reached for a jar.

"You downloaded that app last night, right?" Shane asked.

"I think so."

"I hope so," Shane responded. He looked worried.

"If not, I'll do it as soon as we finish setting up," Nigel reassured his brother. Nigel turned his attention to a second crate filled with candy flavored popcorn. "Mom, where are we going to set up the popcorn?" he asked.

"Over there," Nigel's mom instructed, pointing to the display stands on the table. "You can put the popcorn over there right next to the cupcakes," she said as she pointed to an empty space.

"I'll finish setting up our table," Shane said as he unloaded the remaining desserts. "You go and make sure that payment-processing app is ready."

"I am doing it right now." After a few minutes on his cell phone, Nigel announced proudly, "It works!"

Their first customer approached. "Hey guys," to get their attention.

Shane and Nigel responded as one. "Hello, sir."

"So, what are you selling here?" he asked.

"We have popcorn, cupcakes, and cake jars," Shane answered.

Nigel chimed in. "We have strawberry, coconut, mocha, and banana pudding," as he pointed to the chalkboard signs with the name of each flavor.

"I'll take a strawberry jar. Do you guys accept any payment apps?" the customer asked.

"Yes sir," Nigel gave the customer their payment information.

The customer typed the payment instructions on his cell phone and completed the transaction. "I sent the money to you."

"Thank you, Sir," Nigel responded. "Have a nice day."

The second customer approached.

Nigel greeted her with a smile. "Hello."

"So, what are you selling?" she asked.

"We are selling cake jars…" Shane paused and stared in disbelief. Sibongile Mlambo, the actress from *Lost in Space,* was standing right in front of him. He steadied his nerves and continued to speak. "…and thirty percent of the proceeds go to the JB Dondolo Foundation. Our donation is being designated to help rebuild a hospital in Zimbabwe," Shane explained.

She was impressed. "Thank you so much for supporting The Foundation. They are doing great things over in Zimbabwe. Personally," she began with a smile, "I don't eat sweets, but I would like to donate to The Foundation on your behalf."

"Great," Nigel responded with a broad smile. "Thank you."

"Do you take credit cards?" she asked.

"Sorry, not yet," Nigel explained as his smile faded away.

"Oh! Ok. Let me go get some cash," as she began to walk away.

"We should've gotten a credit card swiper," Shane whispered.

"Yeah, we didn't think about that."

Ms. Sibongile returned with a twenty dollar bill in her hand. "Here you go."

Their third customer approached. "How much do these jars cost?" she asked.

Nigel told her the price.

"Do you guys take credit cards?"

"Sorry, we don't," Nigel responded glumly.

The customer was surprised. "You don't take credit cards?" She paused for a moment. "Okay, I'll go see if any of my friends can lend me some cash."

"Dang, we really should've gotten that credit card swiper," Shane said as he watched the customer walk away.

"I know, good thing some of the people here know each other."

"Yeah, we lucked out."

"I'm back," the third customer announced. "So, what are the flavors?"

Shane perked up. "Strawberry, mocha, banana pudding, and coconut," he responded.

"Ok, I'll take one strawberry jar and one banana pudding jar."

"Hello," the fourth customer greeted as he stood in front of their table holding a credit card in his hand, "Do you take credit cards?" he asked.

"No, Sir," Shane responded.

"Oh, man! I really want to support you guys, but I don't have cash or any of those apps," he said.

Shane couldn't hide his disappointment. "We really should have been ready to accept credit cards."

Definition: To be ready means to anticipate potential problems and glitches, and be prepared to address them successfully. *Unfortunately, my brother and I were not prepared to accept credit cards. Some of the customers were able to borrow money from their friends, but some were not.*

Edible Thought: Some opportunities knock on your door once in a lifetime. Be ready when the knock comes.

CHAPTER 4

DILIGENCE

"Remember when I fell asleep on the stairs…"

"Your dad and I are going out," the boys' mom said. "Ms. Dominique will be here in a few minutes and will stay with you while we're gone. Please keep in mind; she has an exam to study for, so, we need you to be on your A-game. This means taking care of the things we discussed earlier. The most important item on your list is getting ready for your event tomorrow. You need three dozen cupcakes. They can be any flavor. Just make sure you bake THREE dozen. I suggest you start baking around seven-thirty at the latest."

Shane and Nigel bid their mom and dad goodbye. "Okay. Have fun," they said in unison.

As soon as their parents left, they headed upstairs to the game room. They started playing online games with some of their friends.

"Cooper, are you there?" Nigel asked.

"Yeah," Cooper responded.

"Okay. Hang on," Nigel instructed. "I'm going to invite Tino and Gabe to the party."

"Okay."

"Can I join?" Shane asked.

"No," Nigel responded.

"N. I. G. E. L!" Shane insisted.

Nigel chuckled. "I'm joking." After adding a few more players, he said, "Everybody in?"

"Yeah," the boys responded.

"I'll start building our house. Shane and Cooper, you start gathering food. Gabe, you start making weapons. Tino, you... just do what you want."

"Cool," Tino replied.

"How come Tino gets to do what he wants?"

"Because he's new to the game," Nigel responded.

"Ok, I'll start picking tomatoes for some soup."

"I'll make the pot while we're waiting for Gabe to finish the weapons."

"Cooper and I will go get some meat."

"Wait. Our mom is home. What time is it?" Shane asked.

"Yeah, I'll be right back too," Nigel responded as he dropped his headset.

The boys' mom looked around the kitchen and realized that no baking had been done. "Have you guys even started baking?" She already knew the answer.

"Uhh, no," Shane responded.

"You need to get started," their mom directed. "I expected you guys to *at least* have started working on *something*."

"We'll start now," Nigel said humbly.

Shane reached inside the pantry. "I'll get the baking powder."

Nigel yawned and let out a deep breath. "I'm exhausted," he said. "I'm going to sit on the stairs for a minute."

A while later, Shane announced, "I'm almost done with the batter. Nigel, can you start prepping the pan?"

A loud and shallow snuffle came from Nigel's throat.

"Nigel?" Shane called to his brother.

"Zzzzzz."

"Are you sleeping?" Shane asked.

Nigel sat up, stunned. "Uhh. What?"

"Were you asleep?"

"No!" Nigel responded.

"Get up. We need to finish the cake."

"I'm so tired; I can't even think straight. I wish we were done already so I can go to sleep."

Definition: Diligence is working hard and smart. *My brother and I were not diligent in managing our time, which eventually made it hard for us to complete this order.*

Edible Thought: Diligence marks the difference between being good and being great.

CHAPTER 5

STAY IN YOUR LANE

"Remember when I had just separated those egg whites and..."

"**I**'m almost done separating the egg whites," Nigel said as he tediously cracked egg after egg in the palm of his hand and let the whites run through his fingers into the bowl.

"I'm almost done sifting this flour," Shane responded.

Nigel was careful not to overfill the bowl. "Ugh, all the eggs won't fit in here," he grumbled.

Shane finished sifting the flour and immediately grabbed for the bowl with egg whites. The bowl toppled side to side, causing a quarter of the egg whites to spill onto the counter and slide down to the floor.

Frustrated and annoyed, Nigel yelled, "Shane! What are you doing?"

"I thought I could get the remaining egg whites in the bowl."

"I told you they wouldn't fit."

"I was trying to help, based on the Laws of Fluid Mechanics, they all should have fit."

"Well, that *Flu Maniac* or whatever you quoted was wrong because the eggs don't fit," Nigel replied as he reached for another bowl. He finished separating the remaining eggs and added a few extra to account for the ones that spilled.

"Here's your pan," Shane said, still trying to be helpful.

"Gracias," Nigel smiled at his brother.

Definition: "Stay in your lane," is another way of saying, "Don't jump in and take over unless you've been invited." *I jumped into Nigel's workspace without an invitation. My act resulted in wasted supplies and time.*

Edible Thought: Staying in your lane eliminates communication crashes.

CHAPTER 6

KNOW YOUR LIMITS

"Remember when we had to turn down that cake order…"

"Oh, my goodness! Look at this cake order we just received," Shane blurted out.

"What is it?" Nigel asked.

"A cake that looks like a book."

Nigel held his hands up in surrender. "No, I don't think we can do that," as he glanced at the picture.

"It's not that hard."

"Yes, it is," Nigel shot back. "Look at all the intricate details. The spine looks like worn leather, and the pages actually look like they are turning in mid-air."

"C'mon, I bet we can learn how to make it."

"You mean, *you* can learn how to make it?"

"No, you are going to help me," Shane insisted.

"I'm not helping you after you flour-bombed the kitchen the last time!"

"That was an accident. C'mon, I think we can make this cake! Remember the marble glaze cake, the wedding cake, and the succulent cake? You thought we couldn't do those either, but we did."

"I'm right this time," Nigel insisted. "I know I say that on just about every new design we get, and we somehow managed to pull it off, but this time…" He took a second glance at the picture. "…I don't think so. It will also use up a lot of our supplies, time, and energy. I'm not with you on this one," Nigel declared.

"Ugh, I don't like when you're right, but you *may* be right this time," Shane concurred. "Man, I wish…."

"The last thing we want is to have an angry customer," Nigel reminded his brother.

Definition: Knowing your limits includes having a self-awareness of your knowledge and skill set. *Even though we were excited about getting a complicated cake order, we knew it would cost us too much time and money to make this cake, and our customer might not be happy with the end result either.*

Edible Thought: You don't always have to say, "Yes." Sometimes, it is more profitable to say, "No."

CHAPTER 7

WORK ETHIC

"Remember when we stayed up until two o'clock in the morning..."

"Alright, the cake is almost done," Nigel said.

"All we have to do now is to add the green mountains around the bottom," Shane replied.

"Ok."

"This cake looks a little shifty," Shane said anxiously.

"Relax Shane, it's fine."

"Are you sure?"

Nigel's face gleamed with excitement. "Yes, it's fine. I never thought we would be able to make a cake like this. This is definitely the hardest cake we've made so far."

"You think this cake was harder than the wedding cake?"

"Definitely. Let's put it in the box. Ms. Janis should be here soon."

"Okay," Nigel said. "Hold the box still so I can put the cake in."

"Ms. Janis is here," the boys' mother announced.

Nigel and Shane walked into the front room and greeted Ms. Janis.

"I'm looking forward to my cake," she said.

"I know you are going to love it," Nigel responded with a smile.

After everyone exchanged their goodbyes, Ms. Janis left.

"Now, we can go play video games," Nigel blurted out as he danced down the hallway.

Shane and Nigel ran upstairs to the game room.

Thirty minutes later, the boys heard their mom call from downstairs. "Shane. Nigel. Come down, please..."

"What did you say?" the boys called out as they ran down the stairs.

"Ms. Janis just called and said her cake is leaning. We need to go over to her house and take a look at it."

Nigel let out a deep breath and headed upstairs to put on his socks and shoes.

"Dang it," Shane mumbled under his breath.

During the drive over to Ms. Janis' house, the boys' minds raced through all the different scenarios about what may have gone wrong with the cake they just spent *over six hours* making.

"Maybe we didn't use enough dowel rods?" Nigel thought out loud.

"Not sure," Shane responded with a blank look on his face.

"We'll just see for ourselves when we get there," their mom interjected.

As soon as they saw the cake, they couldn't help but notice the top tier was leaning like the Tower of Pisa.

"We will make this right," Shane promised.

"Great! What time can I have it back?" she asked.

"We should be done by ten o'clock tonight. Is that too late?" Nigel asked.

"I'll be up 'till around eleven. Any time before then is fine."

Once they were all in the car, Nigel let out a deep breath. "The cake wasn't as bad as I thought it would be," he said. "I thought the top tier had fallen off."

"Me too," Shane quietly responded.

Back in the kitchen, Shane began barking out instructions. "Alright, so all we have to do is take the top tier of the cake off, add a few more wooden dowel rods to the base, roll out some new fondant, and put the top tier back on the cake."

"Ok."

After Shane carefully removed the fondant, he discovered the problem. "The base on the cake isn't sturdy. We need to bake another cake for the bottom tier."

"Ahhh man," Nigel whined thinking about the amount of time it was going to take for them to make the correction.

"I know. We better text Ms. Janis and let her know that we won't be able to bring the cake until tomorrow morning," Shane said.

"Well, in that case, do we have to remake the cake tonight?" Nigel asked, hoping for a reprieve.

"Sorry guys, you have to make it tonight," the boys' mom chimed in. "Ms. Janis needs the cake first thing in the morning for the baby shower she is hosting."

"Man, we won't get to go to bed until after two o'clock in the morning," Nigel grumbled. He reached for a pair of plastic gloves and blue gel food coloring.

"It should be easier this time because we know how to make it," assured Shane.

"I sure hope so," proclaimed Nigel.

A few hours later, they were ready for the final steps.

"All we have to do now is to stack the cakes," Shane rhapsodized as he finally began showing signs of joy. "Is it just me, or do you think we did a better job this time?"

"I agree. The fondant looks much smoother this time."

Exhausted and drained, the boys finished the cake. "I'm done," Shane sluggishly said.

"Finally," Nigel said. "I'm so tired; I can barely stand. It's almost two o'clock in the morning. I am dying!"

Definition: Work ethic means being diligent and putting your best foot forward until the task is completed. *As tired as we were, we were determined to give Ms. Janis a cake we would be proud of.*

Edible Thought: Sometimes, mistakes can bring about the best lessons in developing a solid work ethic.

CHAPTER 8

FOCUS

"Remember when I made the wrong cake... *twice..."*

Shane smacked his forehead with the palm of his hand. "Ugh, I put coconut extract instead of almond extract in the batter," he said with disappointment.

"Are you serious?" Nigel asked.

"Yes," Shane replied as he sighed.

Nigel tried to keep the conversation positive. "Any way we can fix it?" he asked.

"No, we're going to have to start over," Shane responded disappointedly.

"We might as well go ahead and make the coconut cake too since we have the batter for it already. Dad will be happy," Nigel replied with a smile. "Coconut cake is his favorite. Hmm... You think we can sell him this coconut cake?"

"Nigel!" Shane scolded.

Nigel laughed. "He is always asking for cake scraps anyway. At least, I'll ask. What's that saying? 'If you don't ask, you don't get.'

I am going to text him and see if he wants to buy a coconut cake from us *today*."

"Okay, go ahead," Shane replied.

Five minutes later...

"You are not going to believe this!" Shane exclaimed.

"What?"

"I did it again. I put coconut extract instead of almond extract in the batter," Shane confessed.

"Give me that coconut extract now! I can't believe you actually just made the same mistake *twice*. Some errors are inevitable, but this is not one of those cases."

"I could have used some help," Shane refuted.

"With what? You want me to help you put in the wrong flavoring?" Nigel asked sarcastically.

"I'm having an off day. Cut me some slack."

"Maybe you should've focused more."

"How was I supposed to?" Shane objected.

"I don't know," Nigel responded as he rubbed his chin. "Like, maybe before you started baking, you might have thought, 'I need to concentrate, so I don't make the same mistake *twice*.'"

"You didn't do anything to help either time though," Shane shot back.

"Whatever..." Nigel argued.

"Fine, I'll try to focus more next time."

Definition: Focus means giving your full attention to what you are doing. *Shane did not take the time to focus; therefore, wasting time and energy.*

Edible Thought: Taking a few minutes to gather your thoughts can save you hours of frustration.

CHAPTER 9

RESPONSIBILITY

"Remember when we wanted to buy that thousand-dollar oven..."

Shane and Nigel browsed the aisles of the restaurant supply store. The store was packed with the latest equipment and supplies. "I wonder how much a food prep table will cost," Nigel asked.

"I don't know, but when I was looking online, they were around two-fifty," Shane replied.

"Dang, that's a lot of money. We better choose the right one then," Nigel said as he carefully inspected each table looking for flaws as if he was a Home Owners Association inspector. "Hmm. I think this is the one."

"I'm going to find out how much it cost," Shane said as he turned to go find a salesperson. After going up and down two or three aisles, he spotted a salesperson restocking supplies, "Excuse me, Sir, how much does a thirty-six-inch prep table cost? Oh, and can we add wheels to the table too?"

"Let me go check." The salesman walked away to find the price and additional information about the table.

"While we're here, we might as well go look at some ovens too," Nigel suggested.

"Cool, we need one anyway," Shane agreed.

Nigel pointed to a shiny stainless steel half-size commercial oven. "Look how compact it is…" Reading the label on the oven, "…it uses 'forced air heat-circulation system for even baking.' We could take twice the orders and make twice the money," Nigel said enthusiastically.

"Speaking of money, turn over that tag. How much does it cost?" Shane asked.

Nigel frowned. "Uhh,…a thousand dollars."

"That's a lot of money!" Shane's eyes widened.

"True, but we have enough money in our business checking account," Nigel replied.

"Where would we put it?"

"In the baking room, right beside the mini fridge, so when people pick up their orders, they can see our new oven."

"Good idea. Let's get it."

"We should look online and see what they have there first," Nigel suggested as he pulled his phone from his back pocket. He Googled "commercial ovens."

"The prices are better online than they are here," Nigel said.

"I don't know. Maybe we should wait."

Nigel concurred. "I really want to get this oven though, but if we get it, we will have to get a new table to put the oven on."

"I guess we should wait." Shane looked around the store. "Let's go see how much the table cost."

"Remember, we're only looking to buy *one* table," Nigel reminded his brother.

"I know," Shane responded. "You're the one who was looking at a thousand-dollar oven."

Definition: Responsibility is making wise decisions with the information and resources you have at a given time. *We made a wise decision not to buy the oven because we weren't using our current oven to its full capacity.*

Edible Thought: Being responsible is not always exciting, but the success you achieve for being responsible is exciting.

CHAPTER 10

EFFICIENCY

"Remember when we set up workstations…"

"How in the world are we going to get this order done? Maybe we should have told them we didn't have enough time." Nigel said as a worried look flashed over his face.

"I'm not sure, but we can't waste time or energy like the last time," Shane reflected. "We really need to get more organized. Every time we have a big order, it takes us longer than planned."

Okay, Nigel thought to himself. *Think!*

Shane interrupted his thoughts. "I got it," he interjected.

"You look like you came up with some ridiculous idea," Nigel teased.

"What do mean?" Shane asked, wondering why his brother would make such a comment.

"You always come up with crazy and complicated ideas and say that they're simple," Nigel complained.

Shane was not amused. "Do you want to hear my idea or not?"

"What is it?" Nigel responded as he rolled his eyes.

"*It's simple.* All we have to do is set up different workstations that serve different purposes. Like, we have a station where we prep the pans, another one where we assemble the jars and ..."

"What?" Nigel interrupted as he stared at his brother with amazement, "You actually came up with a simple idea. This is a first…Oh, just FYI, I am not manning the dishwashing station."

The boys proceeded to set up the various workstations.

Definition: Efficiency is using your time and resources in a manner that produces little waste. *Nigel and I knew we had to improve our productivity in order to complete our order within our given deadline.*

Edible Thought: Your level of efficiency will increase the value of your time.

CHAPTER 11

PLANNING

"Remember when you forgot to put eggs and butter on the shopping list..."

The day began with basketball practice at six in the morning where Shane and Nigel put in two hours of basketball drills in preparation for their Regional Tournament in two weeks. After practice, their mom dropped them off at home so they could shower and start baking while she ran to the store to pick up a few ingredients for the day's cake orders.

Shane was first in the kitchen. Unbeknownst to him, Nigel had started playing online video games with his friend, Dean.

"Nigel, are you ready to start baking?" Shane yelled upstairs.

"Uhh, okay," Nigel replied. "Hang on a minute. I'll bake the cake. I just have to log off first."

Once they were in the kitchen, they assumed their usual roles with rhythmic precision. While Nigel began preparing to bake the cake, Shane started making the icing.

"Hey, can you measure out the flour and sugar?" Nigel asked as he opened the fridge.

"Sure," Shane replied.

Nigel searched for eggs and butter, but couldn't find any. "There aren't any eggs or butter in here," he announced.

"What? There should be?" Shane replied with a concerned look on his face.

"There aren't any eggs or butter in the fridge," Nigel repeated.

"Do I have to go the store *again*?" their mom chimed in as she unloaded groceries.

"Yeah," they both responded in unison.

"Yes," their mom said, correcting their grammar. "Who is in charge of inventory management?"

"Nigel," Shane quickly responded.

Nigel turned and shot a *did-you-just-throw-me-under-the-bus?* glance at Shane. "I thought I put everything on the list," Nigel responded as a look of humility washed over his face.

Their mom reached for her purse and keys, looked at Nigel. "This is the second time today that I've had to go to the store, and it's not even noon. Instead of this being a two-hour job, it has turned into a four-hour job," she griped.

Nigel reviewed his list of ingredients and looked in the pantry and the refrigerator. "I am triple-checking to make sure we have the rest of the ingredients." He handed his mother his list. "While you're gone, we'll get everything ready and then, can we get on our electronics for a while since we won't finish baking until after electronic time ends?"

"No, you guys are going with me."

"Why do I have to go?" Shane snarked. "Nigel left the ingredients off of the list, not me."

Their mom simply responded, "Both of you are going."

Definition: Planning is knowing what you're going to do and need *before* you start a task. *Our poor planning delayed the process of completing our cake order.*

Edible Thought: It may take you one hour to plan out something, but it will save you hours of frustration.

CHAPTER 12

COMMUNICATION

"Remember when our cake batter looked like oatmeal ..."

Early Friday morning, Shane and Nigel began baking. They had several orders to fill over the next four days, including a birthday cake for twins who were turning ten, assorted cupcakes for another customer, a coconut cake and a strawberry cake for Ms. Ricks' corporate dinner party, and cakesicles for another birthday party.

"Shane, did you just add flour to the mix?" Nigel asked. He looked concerned.

"Yes," Shane replied.

"Ugh, um! I already added flour," Nigel sputtered as he trashed the bowl of ingredients with the double flour.

"Ohhhh," Shane said, "So, that's why it was so thick and lumpy like oatmeal." He seemed somewhat relieved.

Nigel seemed annoyed. "No one wants a lumpy cake. Now, we'll have to remake it. Let's make sure we get it right this time," he said gloomily.

"We have to pay closer attention next time. It's tiring remaking order after order," Shane replied with a sad tone. He began washing the mixing bowl.

"I'll measure all the dry ingredients, and you do all the wet ingredients."

"Got it."

After Nigel finished measuring all of the dry ingredients, he asked Shane, "What do you want me to do next?"

"Start mixing the sugar and the butter."

They continued measuring and mixing until the batter was ready. Nigel turned on the oven as Shane reached for the pans.

"Man, these pans are heavy," Shane complained.

"No, they're not! You're just W. E. A. K.," Nigel said as he pulled the parchment paper from the pantry. "Here you go," he said as he handed Shane the items needed to prep the cake pans.

Shane oiled and dusted flour on the pans. After he finished prepping the pans, he completed the steps necessary to get the cakes in the oven and set the timer to thirty-five minutes.

"Wow! We got that cake done fast," Nigel said. "I hope it comes out right."

"It will," Shane said as he began piping the icing on the cupcakes they had made earlier. "Grab an icing bag and help me get all of these done."

Definition: Communication is sharing or exchanging information with another individual. *The first batch of the batter had to be thrown away because Shane and I did not communicate the ingredients we each were adding to the mix.*

Edible Thought: Lack of communication reduces morale and efficiency.

CHAPTER 13

GIVING BACK

"Remember when we purchased over two hundred packs of ramen noodles..."

Nigel sat at the table and calculated the day's earnings. "We need to figure out our cupcake sales for the weekend," he prompted. "Remember, we pledged to purchase a case of ramen noodles for every dozen of cupcakes we sold." He reached for the wall calendar and checked for delivery dates.

"Ok," Shane responded, "You call the orders out, and I'll write them down."

"The first order is from Ms. Sharon ... two dozen," Nigel called out.

"Got it," Shane acknowledged as he began writing.

Nigel continued. "One dozen for Ms. Anissa, two dozen for Dr. Wade, two dozen for Aunt Tina, one dozen for Ms. BJ, one dozen for Ms. Ebony, two dozen for Ms. Cathy..."

"Chill, slow down," Shane complained.

Nigel paused to give his brother a chance to write the orders he'd called out. When Shane stopped writing, he started calling out names and numbers again. "...one for Ms. Felicia, one dozen for Ms. Alana and two for the dentist's office."

Shane looked up with a quizzical expression on his face. "The dentist's office? I wonder if Dr. John knows his staff eats *sweets*," he chuckled.

"I know," Nigel laughed. "How many orders does that make?"

Shane counted the orders. "Fifteen dozen," he replied. "This means that we need to buy fifteen cases of noodles to donate to The Prison Ministry."

"I thought we were buying food for the homeless."

"We are. Were you not paying attention during the meeting? Once prisoners are released, unfortunately, quite a number of them end up homeless. So, The Prison Ministry is going to pass out food to the homeless."

"Oh, I see," Nigel responded while shaking his head in agreement.

They gave the list to their mom and asked if she could take them to the grocery store.

"Let's make sure we get the ones in a cup. Get five beef and ten chicken flavor," Nigel instructed.

"That will give us one hundred and fifty individual cups of noodles," Shane responded. "Let's buy five extra cases and bring our total up to two hundred cups."

"Sure!"

A random customer stared and smiled at the cart filled with noodles. "You're not going to go hungry," she joked.

"This isn't for us," Nigel explained. "We're buying these to donate to the homeless."

"Really? It is so nice to see young people who have empathy for others," she responded. She reached in her purse and handed them a crisp twenty dollar bill. "Here," she said, "add some more to your cart."

Shane and Nigel grabbed five more cases and made their way to the front of the store to pay for their order. They got plenty of strange stares along the way.

Definition: Giving back is the act of helping others through sharing one's resources, time, or money. *We used proceeds from our earnings to purchase food for the homeless.*

Edible Thoughts: When giving back to others, make sure you are using a proper measuring cup. Don't be stingy. You will be surprised how the blessings you give to others will come back to you tenfold.

CHAPTER 14

TIME MANAGEMENT

"Remember when it was finals week, and we had a major vendor event…"

"I'll be glad when we break for Christmas," Shane said as he let out a deep and exhausted sigh.

"Me too," Nigel agreed as he flipped through the wrinkled pages of his Algebra 2 textbook. "I'm tired," he said with glazed over eyes. "I don't know how we are going to make it through finals week and bake enough for our event on Saturday."

"Nigel, you're *always* tired. But I'm with you this time," Shane agreed. "The tough part about it is that we can't even start baking until Thursday—three days from now—because we want the cake jars to be fresh. On top of that, I am kind of nervous about my College Algebra final that is on Monday." He stared at the wall. "How are we going to fit everything in?"

Nigel agreed. "I know how you feel. I have a quiz on Monday too. When are we going to find time to study? Man!" He calculated in his head. "There are supposed to be over two hundred people at the event. We could really make some good money and get our name out there at the same time. We are so close to reaching our thousand dollar pledge to the JB Dondolo Foundation. If we sell a hundred jars that gets us three-fourths of the way there."

"On the flip side," Shane reminded his brother, "if we spend too much time baking, and not enough time studying, our grades will suffer."

"*Flip flop*," Nigel gleamed. "That's it! We'll flip flop."

"Flip flop?" Shane responded with a bewildered look on his face.

"Yes. We will flip flop. While you're baking, I'll study. Then I'll step in and assemble the cake in the jars while you study."

Definition: Time management is balancing the time you spend on multiple tasks in a way that allows you to complete each task by its deadline. *To have time to prepare for our event and study, we took turns studying and baking.*

Edible Thought: Manage your time well or your time will manage you.

CHAPTER 15

PERSEVERANCE

"Remember when we wanted to cancel an order…"

"**A**re you crying?" Shane asked when he noticed tears in his brother's eyes.

Nigel let out a deep yawn. "No, I'm just tired," he responded. He glanced at the clock on the stove. *Ugh!* Nigel thought. *It's already eleven-thirty.* "We've been going at it all day."

"Hang in there; We're almost done. All I have to do now is smooth this icing, and we'll be done with this cake," Shane announced. He also yawned deeply. *Yawns are contagious;* he thought to himself as he adjusted his eyes and shook off the sleepiness. No matter how tired he was, he knew the importance of keeping a laser-sharp focus on every cake design. He and his brother would have to push through.

He heard his mom talking in his head. *Every customer deserves your very best every time. Always remember that.* When he finished his last swipe, he sat down the spatula and looked up at Nigel with a tired grin across his face.

"Finally! We're done with all of the orders," Nigel exclaimed as he opened the dishwasher and started loading the last few baking tools.

Shane assembled a cake box.

Hearing the excitement coming from the kitchen, their mom walked in and reminded them to check their orders before they went to bed.

"Ok," Nigel responded, "I'm sure we've got everything." He pressed the 'On' button, shut the dishwasher door, and headed towards the stairs to go to bed.

"Nigel, did you check your orders?" his mom asked again.

"I am doing it right now," Nigel replied as he made an about-face and walked back into the kitchen to review the list. "Ohhh, I forgot the order for mermaid cakesicles," he said with a low, disappointed grumble. They thought about calling the customer early in the morning and canceling the order, but their mom wasn't having it.

Both boys took deep breaths, drank some cold water, wiped their faces, and blinked their eyes as if to summon themselves to wake up.

"Do we have any extra vanilla cupcakes we can use to make cakesicles?" Shane spoke slowly as though he had little energy left.

"Yes."

Nigel reached for a block of white chocolate and a saucepan, "Ok, I'll start melting the chocolate."

"Where is the mold?" Nigel asked.

"In the baking room, on the bottom shelf by the window. Line the mold with the white chocolate. I'll add the cake mixture. After that, we can clean up and go to bed," Shane said.

"Got it," Nigel said. "Hand me that dishcloth."

Shane threw the damp dishcloth at his brother's face. "Here you go."

Nigel was not in the mood for practical jokes. "You didn't have to throw it at my face," he yelled.

"Hahahahaha. That's what you get for leaving out this order."

"Funny," Nigel shot back sarcastically. As he finished the last cakesicle, he said, "Go get the broom."

"No. You go get it. It's right there in the laundry room," Shane bickered back.

"Fine."

"Bring the trash can over here. Hold the dustpan, and we're done."

"Goodnight," Nigel announced as he headed upstairs to his room.

Definition: Perseverance is showing determination in completing a task despite difficulty or delay in achieving success. *Despite how tired we both were, we persevered and got our orders done.*

Edible Thoughts: Life is hard. You must persevere and weed out distractions for your life to blossom.

CHAPTER 16

SALTED CARAMEL

Sunday evening around 6:00

Shane and Nigel's mom took in a deep whiff. The kitchen smelled like vanilla, her favorite scent. She couldn't believe her eyes. *Everything looks great;* she thought to herself as she opened the oven door and examined the interior. It actually sparkled. Wow! They went over and beyond what they'd been asked to do. There were no grease spills on the stovetop and no sticky fingerprints on the pantry door knobs. She walked to the laundry room and found the same condition. The laundry baskets were empty, the ironing board was folded and put away, and the floor had been swept. Even the lint trap on the dryer had been emptied, which is something that rarely happens.

She headed upstairs to the boys' bedrooms. She overheard them in Nigel's room, talking about new ideas for cake flavors.

"What about salted caramel?" Nigel recommended.

"I like it," Shane replied. "That salty-sweet flavor is delicious. And maybe we could use turbinado sugar. That way..."

"Shane. Nigel," their mom exclaimed as she walked into the room, "I am so proud of you two. Wow! You exceeded my expectations. Everything looks and smells amazing."

"Thanks," Shane and Nigel said at the same time.

She handed them a bag which contained their electronics. "Here you go. You are free. You are free to play your games. Thank you for doing even more than I asked. I am very proud of both of you. I love you."

"Love you too, Mom," Nigel replied.

"Love you too," Shane responded as he reached for the controllers.

After their mom left the room, Shane looked at his brother. "Wanna play?"

"Maybe later," Nigel replied. "Let's finish talking about these new flavors first. Oh, don't forget you own me twenty bucks."

ABOUT 2 BROTHERS IN THE KITCHEN

2 Brothers in the Kitchen (2BrosITK)! Well, as our names imply, we are two brothers baking in one kitchen, and we are taking on the baking industry by storm. Don't let our age fool you. We are qualified geniuses not just when facing our love for science and mathematics, we have turned our passion for cooking into an art and have masterminded some desserts that are absolute maximum. Some of our clientele say we should put a "WARNING" sign on our packaging as our desserts are so addictive. So do yourself a favor, and eat every last bite. That way you can go to bed with happy taste buds and no inner turmoil wondering if you should get up and eat the last few bites you were hoping to save to the next day. Go ahead and cake it to the limit.

2BrosITK doesn't just want a world filled with people with happy taste buds. We want people to have happy stomachs and hearts too. That's why we partner with not-for-profit organizations and provide meals for the homeless, toys for children, and funds for medical care.

Honors and Accomplishments

- Featured in Young Entrepreneurs Legancykits.net, Oct 2018

- Young Achievers Award, Zimbabwe Achievers Award, Oct 2018

- Rushion's Spotlight Baker for July 2018

- Featured in Houston Voyage magazine

- Featured in EQT.com magazine

To get in touch with 2 Brothers in the Kitchen for speaking or catering bookings.

Contact Us at:

Website: www.2BrosITK.com

Email: 2BrosITK@gmail.com

Instagram: @2BrosITK

Facebook: @2BrosITK

Twitter: @2BrosITK

Made in the USA
Columbia, SC
02 August 2019